ALEKSANDR ORLOV

PRESENTS

MAIYA

IN THE

Beautiful Ballet

MEERKAT CLASSICS

RUSSIA 2012

Maiya in the Beautiful Ballet
ALEKSANDR ORLOV

1 3 5 7 9 10 8 6 4 2

First published in 2012 by Ebury Press, an imprint of Ebury Publishing

A Random House Group company

The Random House Group Limited Reg. No. 954009

Addresses for companies within the Random House Group can be found at
www.randomhouse.co.uk

A CIP catalogue record for this book is available from the British Library

The Random House Group Limited supports The Forest Stewardship Council
(FSC®), the leading international forest certification organisation. Our
books carrying the FSC label are printed on FSC® certified paper. FSC is
the only forest certification scheme endorsed by the leading environmental
organisations, including Greenpeace. Our paper procurement policy can be
found at www.randomhouse.co.uk/environment

Printed and bound in Italy by Graphicom SRL

ISBN 9780091950040

To buy books by your favourite authors and register for offers visit
www.randomhouse.co.uk

A MESSAGE FROM THE AUTHOR

Now here is something specials.

This is the story of very talented person, who in real life hide her light in the bushel. But here we are lift up bushel and see the talent.

Sometimes I expect you think your teacher is not very interesting. Well, let me be telling you, Miss Maiya is not only very interesting she is also very beautiful and has extra special brilliance.

She may seem strict when she teach the little meerpups of Meerkovo but she is actually full of artistry.

Please be admirings.

Yours,

ALEKSANDR ORLOV

It was six o'clock on Saturday night.

In Vitaly Square, in the middle of Moscow, there is great excitements. In one hour curtain will go up on the stage of Russian Imperial Theatre.

It is first night of the famous ballet **"Romeero and Juliet".** Tickets to see it cost hundreds of roubles. There is big crowd waiting to go in – they are dressed in their best and very excite.

Here is actual pair of tickets for opening night. They were so hot they could fry the fur on your paws!

Inside the theatre, behind the biggest dressing-room door with the biggest star on it, was the biggest dressing-room. In it there were many many bunch of flowers. And in middle of all was
Maiya, Prima Ballerina of all Russia.

She was dress in her world-famous green tutu and her lucky ballet pumps (the ones with green ribbons). She look in mirror to make sure her fur was fluffy and her nose shiny.*

*A shiny nose is a success nose, as my great granddaddy always say.

As she gaze at herself in mirror, Maiya remember all those years of longing to be famous ballet dancer.

She was wanting to be dancer right from days of being meerpup in little village of Meerkovo. When she was tiny she would sneak into the Orlov family mansion. When no one was looking she would spend many hours practising her arabesques in the private mirrored ballroom.*

*This was naughty because ballroom only for balls and not for pup dancing practice. But I think owner of Orlov family mansion would not be very cross.

Now, after practise for hours every day for years, her dreams were come true. Soon she would be on stage with the brilliant dancer Aleksandrovic Orlovski, who was most handsome and talent dancer ever to be on stage.

She was very excite to be dancing with him, not just because of his **great handsomeness** (he look fantastic in tights) but also because he has strong arms for better throwing in the air.* Maiya has to do the triple pirouette jump in this ballet, which is difficult and dangerous, so she need partner with great strength.

See how complicated is the triple pirouette?
All that throwing and turning and rushing – incredibles!

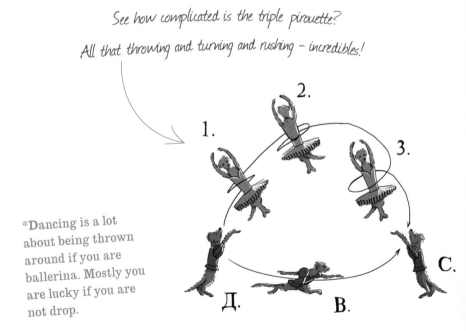

1.
2.
3.
Д.
В.
С.

*Dancing is a lot about being thrown around if you are ballerina. Mostly you are lucky if you are not drop.

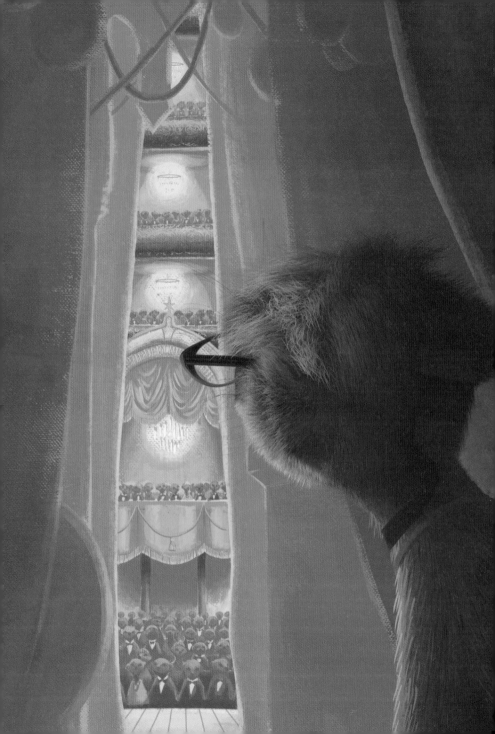

Maiya was very nervousness.
But she knew you had to be nervousness to do your best.
In the distance she could hear orchestra tuning up.

It was nearly time...

She start the walk through the passages backstage at
the theatre. She can see lines and lines of expectant faces
in the audience. It is all very daunt.

The orchestra tuning gets louder and now she can see the
world-famous conductor Sergeinini.

He is very old now, and very grey, and he has to sit down a
lot. But Maiya was glad he was in charge because he was very
careful in his conducting, and, so long as he stay awake and
not fall off his stool, he was the best.

*Seating plan for theatre show how even the little peoples
in the balcony have excellent view.*

Maiya stepped out on stage.

As the music start, the audience is complete
hush and all attention.

She start to pirouette towards centre of stage
and then from other side appear Aleksandrovic himself.

He was look his best. Dressed from head to paw
in pure handsomeness, his cravat twinkle in the lights.

Here is costumes for
Romeero and Juliet.
I am sure you don't need me
to tell you which one is which!

Maiya try not to be distract by his handsomeness.
With one delicate turn she fall into his arms and he lift her
high into the air.

Faster and faster goes the music. They leap higher
and higher as they turn and twirl.*

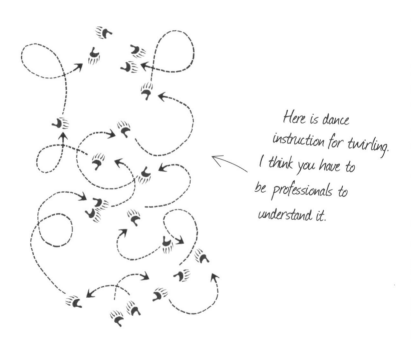

Here is dance
instruction for twirling.
I think you have to
be professionals to
understand it.

*Twirling can make for giddy. As Sergei know when he fall
over trying to do ballroom dance.

They are dance like they have never dance before. Maiya loves the
feel of Aleksandrovic's strong arms around her, and the feel
of his breath on her fur. It make her glasses go all steamy.

And still there is the triple pirouette jump
to come. It is **crowning point
of whole ballet**, but Maiya
wonder if she have strength left
for such difficultness.

Now is the moment.

Together they rush to the left of the stage.
Then they rush to the right of the stage.
(There is a lot of rush in ballet).
And then Maiya leaps into the air.

She turns once, then twice. Time stand
still. The audience is hold its breath.
Then with one more turn she lands
on stage with delicate grace. She looks
at Aleksandrovic in triumphant and
together they turn and twirl again.

Then it is all over, and they are stand at the front of the stage bowing and bowing.

"Bravo!
     Bravo!" cry the audience.

They stamp their paws on the floor with a din that is thunderous.

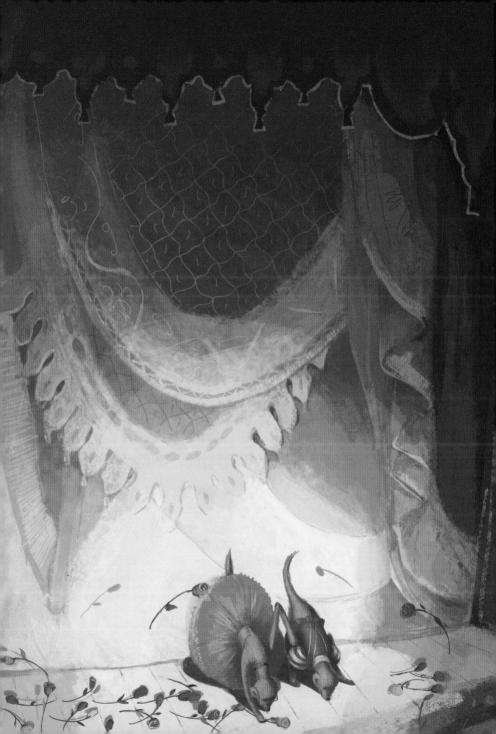

The din got louder and louder until – it sound just like Bogdan and the meerpups of year 4.

It *was* Bogdan and the meerpups of year 4! And they are heading towards their classroom.

After one last brilliant pirouette the breathless Maiya stop dancing and found herself stand by her familiar teacher desk. It was time for another arithmetic lesson.

Just before the door of the classroom opened she glance at the poster on wall behind her. The picture of the beautiful ballet dancer in the green tutu is a bit fadey now, but there was no mistaking the green ribbons.

Aleksandr's Life Lesson

Talent and beauty can be lurk behind stern exteriors.

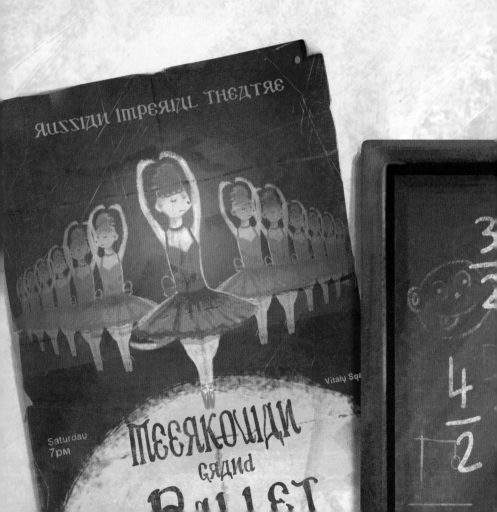

Now read my other greatest tales

Available from all good bookshops

Also available to download as an ebookamabob
or audiomajig as read by the author – me!

For more information visit www.comparethemeerkat.com